GRAPHIC HISTORY

THE CURSE OF KING TUT'S TOMB

by Michael Burgan
illustrated by Barbara Schulz

Consultant:
Carolyn Graves Brown
Curator, Egypt Centre, University of Wales Swansea
Swansea, Wales

Raintree

www.raintreepublishers.co.uk
Visit our website to find out
more information about
Raintree books.

To order:
☎ Phone 0845 6044371
🖨 Fax +44 (0) 1865 312263
🖳 Email myorders@raintreepublishers.co.uk

Customers from outside the UK please telephone +44 1865 312262

Raintree is an imprint of Capstone Global Library Limited, a company incorporated in England and Wales having its registered office at 7 Pilgrim Street, London, EC4V 6LB – Registered company number: 6695582

Text © Stone Arch Books 2005
First published in the United Kingdom by Capstone Global Library 2010
Paperback edition first published in the United Kingdom by Capstone Global Library in 2011
The moral rights of the proprietor have been asserted.

Art Directors: Jason Knudson & Heather Kindseth
Storyboard Artists: Jason Knudson & Sandra D'Antonio
Colourist: Ben Hunzeker
Editor: Amanda Doering
UK Editor: Vaarunika Dharmapala
Originated by Capstone Global Library Ltd
Printed and bound in China by South China Printing Company Ltd

Acknowledgments
We would like to thank Philip Charles Crawford for his assistance in the preparation of this book.

ISBN 978 1 406214 34 5 (hardback)
14 13 12 11 10
10 9 8 7 6 5 4 3 2 1

ISBN 978 1 406214 39 0 (paperback)
15 14 13 12 11
10 9 8 7 6 5 4 3 2 1

British Library Cataloguing in Publication Data
A full catalogue record for this book is available from the British Library.

Disclaimer
All the Internet addresses (URLs) given in this book were valid at the time of going to press. However, due to the dynamic nature of the Internet, some addresses may have changed, or sites may have changed or ceased to exist since publication. While the author and publishers regret any inconvenience this may cause readers, no responsibility for any such changes can be accepted by either the author or the publishers.

Editor's note: Direct quotations from primary sources are indicated by a yellow background.

Direct quotations appear on the following pages:

Pages 9, 11, 14 from *The Tomb of Tutankhamen, Discovered by the Late Earl of Carnarvon and Howard Carter* by Howard Carter and A. C. Mace (Cassell and Company, 1923)

Page 22 from *The Complete Tutankhamun: The King, the Tomb, the Royal Treasure* by Nicholas Reeves (Thames and Hudson, 1990)

CONTENTS

CHAPTER 1

THE MUMMY'S CURSE IS BORN

More than 5,000 years ago there was a rich and powerful kingdom along the Nile River in Egypt. The rulers of this kingdom were called pharaohs.

The Egyptians built huge pyramids and underground tombs, where the pharaohs were buried after they died.

The Egyptians believed that the pharaohs' spirits lived on after death. The tombs held all the things the spirits might need to use in the afterworld.

The Egyptians mummified the dead so that their spirits could return to their bodies. Some of the pharaoh's organs were removed and placed in jars that were left in the tomb.

Egyptian priests cast spells over the dead pharaoh's body. They wound strips of cloth around it, and placed precious stones in the cloth. Writings on the wall warned grave robbers not to disturb the tomb.

May these spells and magical stones protect your spirit forever. May the great god judge anyone who steals from this tomb.

5

What do you think is inside? Gold? Jewels?

Probably just dust from old bones. He's been dead for more than 3,000 years.

I've heard mummies are cursed. We should leave the dead alone.

The idea of a mummy's curse spread. But this did not stop archaeologists from exploring the tombs.

One of these archeologists was Howard Carter. During the early 1900s, he worked in the Valley of the Kings in Egypt for Lord Carnarvon. Lord Carnarvon was deeply interested in Egyptian artefacts.

CHAPTER 2

AN AMAZING DISCOVERY

Three weeks later, Carter and his men had cleared the passage to a sealed doorway. Beyond this, another sealed doorway stood outside King Tut's tomb. Lord Carnarvon waited anxiously for the plaster to be removed.

This doorway has been opened and sealed before. Grave robbers must have found it centuries ago.

There may be nothing left inside.

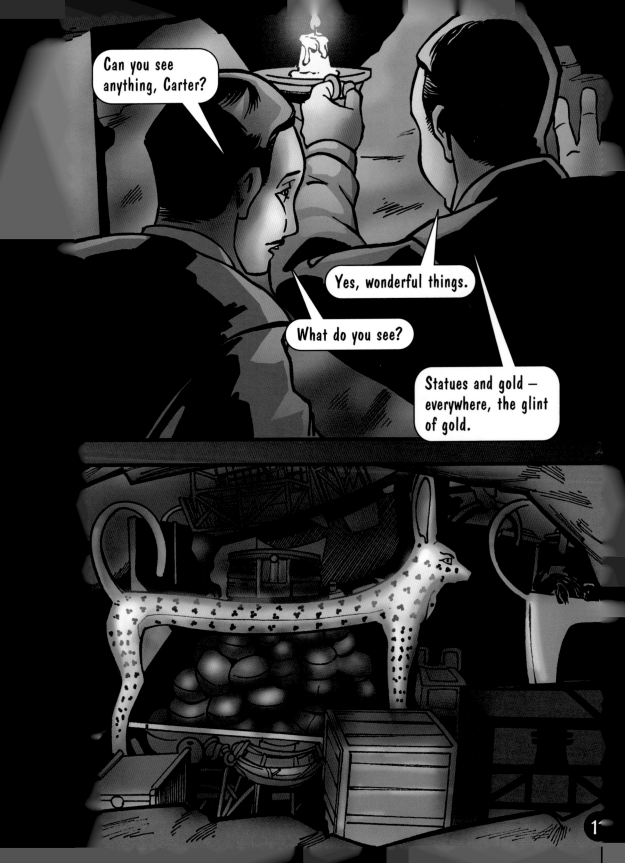

And at the far end of one of the rooms . . .
Statues of Tut himself!
They're like guards protecting his tomb.

In February 1923, the workers broke through another sealed doorway in the tomb. This door led them into the burial chamber.

Look at this beautiful work, Carter. There must be incredible treasures inside.

Yes, and the mummy of King Tut.

We are treading where no one has entered since the boy king was laid to rest nearly 3,300 years ago.

The world followed daily newspaper stories of the excavation of Tut's tomb. Carter and Carnarvon became famous.

Read all about it! More treasures found in Egypt!

THE TIMES
CARTER FINDS TREASURE

CHAPTER 3

THE CURSE AT WORK

Marie Corelli, a famous writer from New York, heard about Carnarvon's poor health. It reminded her of something she had read in an old book about ancient Egypt.

It says here that there was writing outside Tut's tomb that read, "Death shall come on swift wings to him who touches the tomb of the pharaoh."

Did the mosquito bite make Lord Carnarvon ill, or was it caused by a mummy's curse?

Archaeologist Hugh Evelyn-White had been one of the first people to enter the tomb. He hung himself after writing a suicide note in his own blood.

Millionaire George J. Gould died of pneumonia the day after he visited the tomb.

Egyptologist Georges Bénédite died after falling down the stairs of the tomb.

The strange deaths continued.

I HAVE SUCCUMBED TO A CURSE WHICH FORCES ME TO DISAPPEAR

Mr Carter, what do you think of the curse of Tutankhamen?

All sane people should dismiss such inventions with contempt.

Despite talk of the curse, Carter and his crew continued their difficult work in the tomb. Carter's long-time friend Arthur Callender helped him every step of the way.

Callender, this is the coffin of King Tutankhamen. Inside lies the body of the ancient pharaoh.

It's more beautiful than I had imagined. Look at all that gold.

Then, on 11 November 1925, after carefully opening three golden coffins stacked inside each other . . .

Behold, the mummy of King Tut.

Upon unwrapping the mummy, a wound was found on Tut's left cheek.

The wound on Tut's cheek is in the same spot as Carnarvon's mosquito bite!

Some people took this discovery as more evidence of a curse.

Even though the curse hadn't affected Carter or Callender, some people still believed it was real. Herbert Winlock, an expert on ancient Egypt, set out to prove the believers wrong.

	NUMBER OF PEOPLE ATTENDING	NUMBER OF PEOPLE WHO DIED WITHIN 10 YEARS
OPENING OF BURIAL CHAMBER	26	6
UNWRAPPING OF MUMMY	10	0

The numbers don't lie, gentlemen. The people who died were mostly older people, or people already in poor health. The only curse at work is that all people eventually die. Life killed these poor souls, not a mummy's curse.

The reports of strange events related to Tut's tomb stopped. But every so often, a new story was added to the curse's legend.

In 1966, Mohammed Ibrahim, Egypt's director of antiquities, dreamed he would face great danger if Tut's artefacts left Egypt.

No! Noooooo!

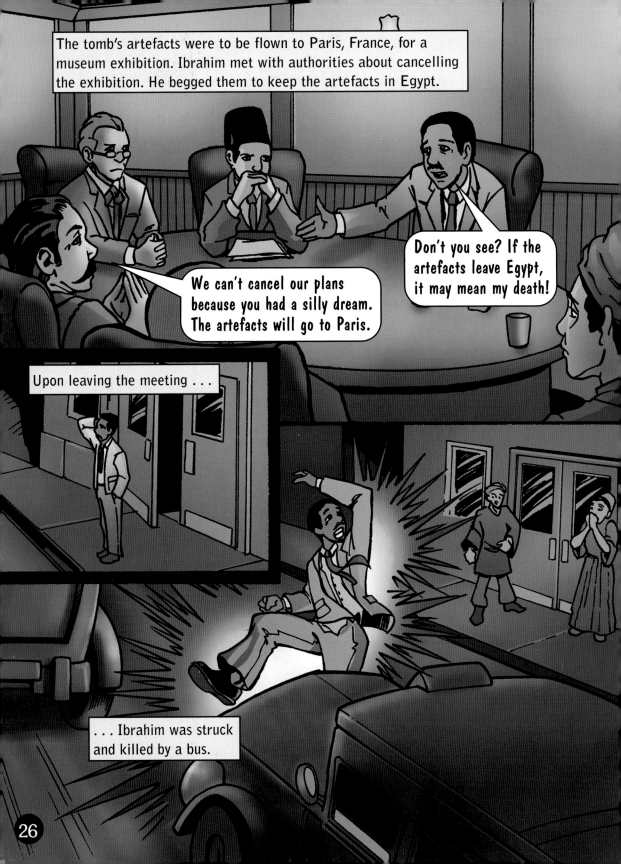

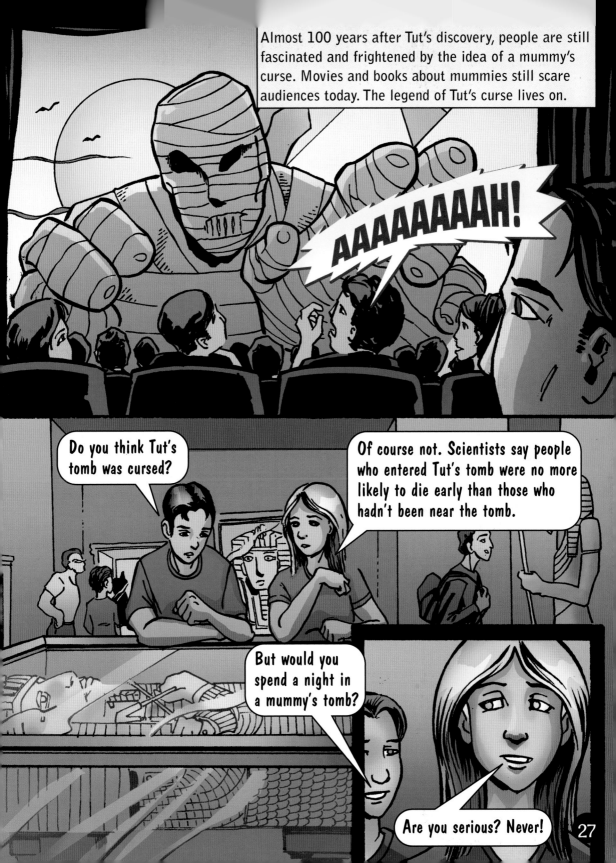

◄ Many people connected with King Tut's tomb died in strange ways. It is not surprising that their deaths were thought to be the result of a curse. For example, the death of Richard Bethell, Howard Carter's personal secretary, caused two more deaths. Bethell's father, Lord Westbury, killed himself after hearing of his son's death. Then, the car carrying Lord Westbury's body to the cemetery struck and killed an eight-year-old boy.

◄ King Tut was buried in a tomb meant for someone else. Other ancient Egyptians' names appear on many of the artefacts left in Tut's tomb. Even one of the coffins he is buried in has someone else's name on it.

◄ Grave robbers probably broke into Tut's tomb shortly after he died. They were caught before much damage was done. Priests reburied the entrance to Tut's tomb, and it stayed buried until Carter found it in 1922.

◄ Howard Carter was more concerned with getting the treasures from Tut's tomb than in preserving the body. Carter cut Tut's body into three pieces. Today, Tut's body lies in his original burial place. It is protected by the Egyptian government.

Howard Carter found the mummies of two of King Tut's children in the king's tomb. Scientists think both children were girls.

Lord Carnarvon had a three-legged dog. It is said that at the exact moment of Lord Carnarvon's death in Cairo, his dog began barking furiously, then suddenly dropped dead too!

Scientists believe that some people who entered Tut's tomb died because of a mould that grew in the tomb. Many kinds of harmful bacteria have been found in Tut's tomb.

Some scientists believe King Tut was murdered. He was only 18 or 19 when he died. X-rays of Tut's skull show that he suffered a blow to the back of his head. He was buried very quickly. The next ruler removed all records of Tut from official documents.

GLOSSARY

archaeologist scientist who studies the past by looking at old buildings and objects

artefact object made by humans that was used in the past. Tools and weapons are artefacts.

Egyptologist someone who studies the language, history, and culture of ancient Egypt

excavation search for ancient remains buried in the ground

mummify preserve a dead body from decay

spirit part of a person thought to control thoughts and feelings. Ancient Egyptians believed the spirit left the body after death and travelled to the afterworld.

INTERNET SITES

http://www.bbc.co.uk/history/ancient/egyptians/tutankhamen_gallery.shtml

On this website, you can have a look at some great pictures of the treasures found in King Tut's tomb.

http://www.britishmuseum.org/explore/families_and_children/online_tours/journey_into_the_mummy/journey_into_the_mummy.aspx

Take an online tour to see a 3,000-year-old mummy unwrapped!

http://www.bbc.co.uk/history/historic_figures/tutankhamen.shtml

This website gives you information about King Tut's life, achievements, and death.

READ MORE

Eyewitness: Ancient Egypt (Dorling Kindersley, 2009)

Hands-on History: Ancient Egypt, Alexandra Fit (Heinemann Library, 2007)

Time Travel Guides: Ancient Egypt, Liz Gogerly (Heinemann Library, 2007)

Virtual History Tours: Look Around an Egyptian Tomb, Liz Gogerly (Franklin Watts, 2007)

BIBLIOGRAPHY

The Tomb of Tut-Ankh-Amen, Discovered by the Late Earl of Carnarvon and Howard Carter, Howard Carter and A. C. Mace. (Cassell and Company, 1923)

Mummies, Myth, and Magic in Ancient Egypt, Christine El Mahdy, (Thames and Hudson, 1989)

Entering King Tut's Tomb, 1922. EyeWitness to History, http://eyewitnesstohistory.com/tut.htm.

Discovery Channel: King Tut – Ask the Experts, Mike King and Greg Cooper, http://dsc.discovery.com/anthology/unsolvedhistory/kingtut/experts/read.html

The Complete Tutankhamun: The King, the Tomb, the Royal Treasure, Nicholas Reeves (Thames and Hudson, 1990)

INDEX